# MARY ENGELBREIT'S

# THE WORLD IS YOURS

**HARPER**
*An Imprint of HarperCollinsPublishers*

Mary Engelbreit's The World is Yours
Copyright © 2019 by Mary Engelbreit Enterprises, Inc.
All rights reserved. Manufactured in China.

www.harpercollinschildrens.com
Library of Congress Control Number: 2018959284
ISBN 978-0-06-288994-2

19  20  21  22  23  SCP  10  9  8  7  6  5  4  3  2  1
❖
First Edition

For Mikayla, who is already
taking the world by storm!

"When I stopped being prisoner to others' opinions of me, I became more confident and free."

—Lucille Ball

"You are fortunate that
you start with nothing to
hold you back, and only a bright
future to beckon you forward."

—Indira Gandhi

"Never flinch,
never weary,
never despair."

—Winston Churchill

"Do not allow yourselves to be disheartened by any failure as long as you have done your best."

—Mother Teresa

"I made up my mind
to try. I tried and I
was successful."

—Bessie Coleman

"Fall down seven times,
get up eight."

—Japanese Proverb

"Success is not alone in skill
and deeds of daring great.
It's in the rose that you plant
beside your garden gate."

—Edgar Albert Guest

"I'm not afraid of
storms, for I'm learning
how to sail my ship."

—Louisa May Alcott

"Instead of falling apart ...
come together."

—Eleanor Roosevelt

"Hold fast to dreams."

—Langston Hughes

"The time to be happy is now, and the way to be happy is to make others so."

—Robert Green Ingersoll

"The only way to endure the
quake is to adjust your stance."

—Oprah Winfrey

"This above all: to thine
own self be true."

—William Shakespeare

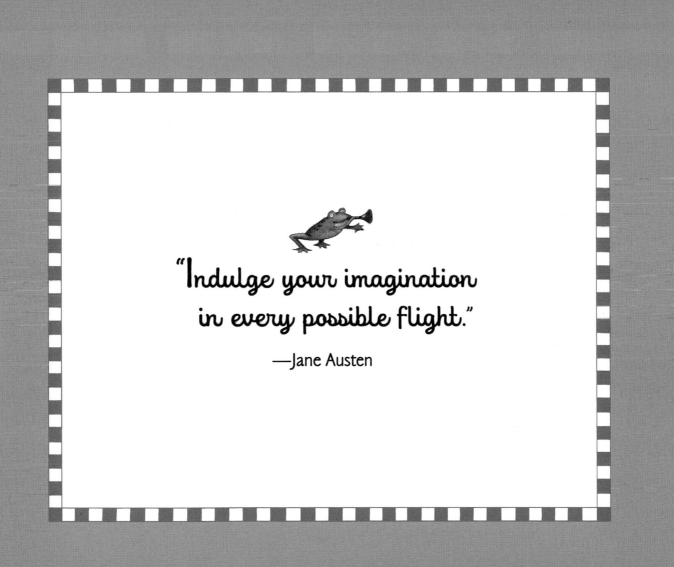

"Indulge your imagination
in every possible flight."

—Jane Austen

"There's only one rule
you need to remember:
laugh at everything."

—Anne Frank

"We may encounter many defeats,
but we must not be defeated."

—Maya Angelou

"If you have two friends in
your lifetime, you're lucky.
If you have one GOOD friend,
you're more than lucky."

—S. E. Hinton

"You want to be the pebble
in the pond that creates
the ripple for change."

—Tim Cook

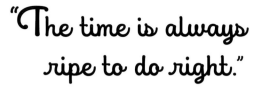

"The time is always ripe to do right."

—Martin Luther King Jr.

"Nothing was useful
which was not honest."

—Benjamin Franklin

"We must not allow fear
to stand in our way."

—Nelson Mandela

"Alone we can do so little;
together we can do so much."

—Helen Keller

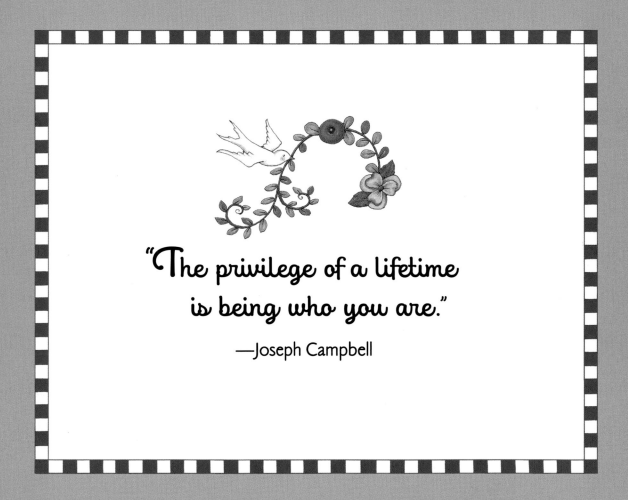

"The privilege of a lifetime
is being who you are."

—Joseph Campbell